Sylvia Lermann

Get Rosacea Under Control Immediately

Practical Guide

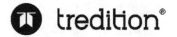

Copyright © 2017 Sylvia Lermann

Publisher: tredition, Hamburg, Germany

ISBN
Paperback: 978-3-7323-9592-7
eBook: 978-3-7323-9593-4

Printed on demand in many countries

Table of contents

Book description

Thank you and congratulations for finding the book "Get Rosacea Under Control Immediately". This book contains tried and tested methods which allow you to get the chronic inflammatory skin disorder rosacea rapidly under control.

Many people around the world, including me, suffer from rosacea. As the doctors were unable to help, I began to do my own research and eventually found the solution.

Now I would like to share what I've learned and provide a practical guide in this book which will allow you to enjoy healthy and beautiful skin.

With the help of a few easy-to-implement measures, your quality of life will soon improve once again.

I wish you every success!

Introduction

This book is a practical guide for sufferers of rosacea, with the help of which they can easily get this skin disorder under control. This guide is the result of intensive research, the results of which I am happy to share with my readers to free them from the "curse of the Celts".

I am not receiving any compensation from the companies and products mentioned in this book; they are merely helpful, concrete recommendations for you, as they have freed me from rosacea.

What is rosacea?

Rosacea (derived from the Latin word *rosaceus* for "rose-coloured") is an inflammatory skin disease which occurs in both genders, predominantly between the ages of 30 and 50, with women being slightly more likely to develop the disorder. As a rule, the disorder develops in stages. It is chronic and is considered to be incurable.

The disorder is usually seen in the middle of the face: the cheeks, nose, chin and forehead are often affected. The typical changes of the skin can also be seen in the neck and décolletage, though this is rare. The area around the mouth and eyes usually remain free of the disorder. Different forms and/or stages of rosacea differ depending on the characteristics of the disorder and the stages do not necessarily overlap.

Rosacea erythemato-teleangiectatica is the first stage of rosacea. The skin reddens when exposed to heat, cold, and during situations of emotional stress, with clearly visible, dilated blood vessels near the skin's surface. The cheeks and nose are particularly affected. The skin looks like it is sunburnt, with a burning or sticky feel, sometimes itchy, and small papules (raised swelled spots) can occur. Early on, the redness will disappear, but in later stages of the disease it can become permanent.

Rosacea papulopustulosa is the second stage of the disease, which can last for several years. In addition to the redness and vasodilatation, there are nodules and pimples as well as swelling which can become inflamed and fester over long periods of time. The disorder may now resemble acne, but the nodules and pimples do not originate in the hair follicles.

In the third stage of rosacea, **rosacea hypertrophica,** the connective tissue and sebaceous glands become increasingly intertwined. Men will experience a knotted thickening of the nose (rhinophyma) develops at this stage. Rarely, comparable skin growths occur on the ear, chin, nasal root or eyelids.

There is also a form of rosacea in which the eyes are affected (ophthalmic rosacea). In addition to dry eyes, various eye infections can occur. Thus, the conjunctiva, the edges of the eyelids, and the iris can become inflamed. Rarely, the cornea can be affected by inflammation. This can even lead to blindness.

The skin damaged by rosacea is extremely sensitive and irritable. It is often very sensitive to skin care preparations, cosmetics and medicines, which make the inflammation worse. Patients suffer and feel increasingly impaired in their quality of life, as the symptoms are on their face, and therefore visible to everyone. Those who consult dermatologists usually get the same answers: rosacea is not curable, and Metrocreme and antibiotics will be prescribed. If these agents help at all, the inflammation will flare up once again after discontinuation of the antibiotics at the latest. So, it was time to find a more long-lasting, quick-acting solution, and I would like to tell you about it in this book, in order to save you from your suffering and help you to restore your healthy skin quickly.

Causes of rosacea

Many different theories try to explain the causes of rosacea.

Most theories refer to the external symptoms: spotty, partly scaly redness, swelling of the facial skin as well as inflamed papules and pustules, and telangiectasia, i.e. the small visible blood vessels. Several possible causes have been discussed, starting with defects in the immune system, the nervous system and the blood vessels in the face, to the sudden multiplication of microbes and demodex mites that live in the hair follicles. There are even suspicions that the tendency to develop the disease could be hereditary, and genetic examinations are currently being performed. I do not wish to go into the various theories, but rather, to point to new scientific findings regarding a hitherto underestimated cause. Here, I am talking about the microscopically small hair follicle mites, which can be found in and on the body of adult humans.

The hair follicle mite is a 0.3-0.4 mm large, ocular human ectoparasite, which lives in the hair follicles and sebaceous glands, especially on the face (nose, chin, eyelids) of most adults. It belongs to the natural inhabitants of the skin and colonizes the hair follicles above the sebaceous glands, especially those in the face. Its related species, demodex brevis is somewhat shorter at 0.15-0.2 mm, and prefers the sebaceous glands as its habitat. They are not visible to the human eye, but under the microscope you can see their worm-like shape with 8 legs. They move at 8-16 mm/hour, preferably at night. When it is light, they retreat into the follicle.

While newborns are still unaffected by these mites, mite colonization increases throughout the course of life, and is present at a rate of 100% in 70-year olds, but mostly at low population densities. [1] "There is no prophylaxis for the demodex infestation, as demodex mites belong to the normal regional flora." [2]

---

[1] Clifford E. Desch: Human hair follicle mites and forensic acarology. In: Experimental and Applied Acarology. Vol. 49, No. 1/2, 2009, pp. 143-146, doi:10.1007/s10493-009-9272-0.
[2] Jansen T, Plewig G: Demodex mites and their importance for facial dermatoses. Munich Med. Weekly 1996; 138: 483-487

Usually the infection remains unnoticed, as it only when a particularly high mite density is reached, that bacteria in the faeces of the mites can cause skin problems, report scientists in the *Journal of Medical Microbiology*. If the mites die, the bacteria are released into the skin tissue, where they contribute to tissue degradation and promote inflammatory processes. The defence cells, which migrate into the affected skin area, emit messenger substances. These in turn cause the vessels to expand. As a result of the inflammation, the cells of the connective tissue and sebaceous glands divide far more frequently than usual. Nodules and pus form, the skin is thickened in places and it also has a coarse-pore appearance.

Factors that dilate the vessels favour the symptoms of rosacea or may aggravate them. These include, for example, stress, alcohol ,or spicy food.

These findings are consistent with my experience and the research results of Irish scientists. A bacterium that is found in the common hair follicle mite demodex folliculorum, which lives on our skin, could be the cause of rosacea.[3]

Here you can see a demodex folliculorum mite, which lives in a human hair follicle.

https://www.youtube.com/watch?v=KfLIn_X1Xx0

These new findings open up new approaches for more targeted treatment. rosacea has been treated with various antibiotics for some time, although no specific bacterial cause has yet been found. Now scientists are able to treat the skin disease more specifically by focusing on the hair follicle mite and a known bacterium.

---

[3] Publication of results: Lacey N, Delaney S, Kavanagh K, Powell FC. Mite-related bacterial antigens stimulate inflammatory cells in rosacea. British Journal of Dermatology 2007;157:474-481.

What the doctor recommends

Now, here is my personal story: My skin was always healthy in the past, and I have been using creams to care for and moisturise it since I was a teenager. As the decades advanced, my peers started to get wrinkles, but I didn't. Everything can be controlled through good care - I thought. But a few years ago, my facial skin suddenly started to turn red and burned more and more every day. Aha, I could no longer tolerate my favourite cream, I thought, and I switched to less perfumed, milder creams. After so many attempts at using different creams and lotions that I became a permanent guest at the pharmacy, it turned out that the inflammation did not fade away even when I used only the mildest creams.

As I did not know what caused this sudden sensitivity, the inflammation itself could barely be concealed with make-up, and I was asking myself however could I manage to get the whole thing under control and my beautiful skin back, I fell into a panic and made an appointment with a renowned dermatologist. As this doctor is considered to be an authority in his field, it took 6 weeks before we finally sat down opposite each other for a consultation. In the meantime, small pimples had formed on my face, and I was close to despair.

The doctor took a large magnifying glass, took one look at my skin and said only "rosacea"! I had heard the word before in connection with the reddened noses of older men. The doctor replied "You mean a rhinophyma, which is the third stage of rosacea. " My fear was now running deep. "Is it curable?" was, of course, my next question. The doctor muttered a short, "no", and bent down over his prescription block. He prescribed me Metrocreme 0.75%, on which I naturally placed high hopes, and within two minutes I was again out on the street.

When I arrived home, I sat down and googled rosacea, and I read many desperate comments in forums, written by people who had sometimes not even left the house for ten years because they were so ashamed of their facial flushing. I could not let things go that far, as I had taken care of my skin so well for decades. So, I used the prescribed Metrocreme, and I followed the application instructions to the dot for several weeks. Every day I looked curiously and hopefully at my skin to see if it had improved. Unfortunately, I saw none at all. There was no improvement in sight. The dermatologist had also prescribed an antibiotic for me, Oraycea (active ingredient doxycycline, made by Galderma).

Antibiotics such as doxycycline are anti-inflammatory and soothing. The doxycycline in Oraycea is such a low dosage that it works against the inflammation, but is does not work as an antibiotic. The normal bacterial fauna hardly changed and it did not cause any superinfections, such as the vaginal Candidiasis.

After I had read in the forums that though the skin improved while taking Oraycea, the inflammation flared up again afterwards, I decided not to use the antibiotic.

As the cream prescribed by the dermatologist did not work after I had tried it a long period of time, I made another attempt to get medical treatment and arranged an appointment with a private dermatologist. This doctor immediately advised me once again to use the said Metro-creme, a suggestion which, after my negative experiences, I rejected, of course. Unfortunately, she did not know of any creams which were more effective than Metrocreme. She said, however, that rosacea could be related to the bacterial climate in the intestines.

So, she prescribed me Perenterol and lactic acid cultures for the intestinal flora. I also took these obediently for a certain period, but I could not see a positive effect. Another dermatologist gave me a skin cream which made my skin greasy and shiny and really clogged up.

After my doctor's odyssey, I felt very alone and desperate. I did not want to accept the fact that I would have to face the world with a red, inflamed face for the rest of my life.

On the evening in which I had searched for the 4th doctor, I sat down at the computer and began to trawl the Internet for treatment options. I was shaken when I read the stories of the many chronic rosacea sufferers, some of whom no longer had the confidence to be around other people.

In the forums, you exchanged stories, gave each other tips for mild creams, which did not inflame the skin even more and talked about plants, whose names I had never heard before. There was still a lot to read about and to try out!

Plants with healing properties

In several forums, I read that the plants Gotu kola and Brahmi are used in Ayurvedic medicine to treat acne, allergies and skin diseases of all kinds.

Gotu kola belongs to the Umbelliferae family and has the botanical name Centella asiatica. Gotu kola is commonly named the Asian pennywort, or the Indian pennywort.

Gotu kola is a creeping herb that is traditionally used mainly to improve mental performance. It is also used to balance the nervous system, and is used internally for wounds, chronic skin diseases, malaria, sexually transmitted diseases, ulcers and varicose veins, nervous disorders and senility. It is used externally to treat wounds, haemorrhoids and rheumatoid arthritis.

There are many other traditional applications. Investigations have shown that Gotu kola can relieve venous discomfort. The active substances support the construction of connective tissue, lymphatic tissue, blood vessels and mucosa. [4]

In China there is a legend, according to which a plant-healer lived to 200 years old by taking Gotu kola. The triterpenoids contained in the plant have been shown to have a healing effect, meaning that Gotu kola can be used externally for burns or various skin diseases.

Gotu kola application and effects

The brahmosides contained in Gotu kola have a soothing and anabolic effect. A few leaves taken fresh daily will significantly lower blood pressure. Gotu kola can be taken as tea, tincture or powder. In Ayurveda medicine, you can drink a maximum of 2 cups a day or use 30 drops of the effective tincture.

---

[4] http://www.ncbi.nlm.nih.gov/pubmed/11666121

Brahmi

Brahmi is a small, creeping, herbaceous plant belonging to the Scrophulariaceae family, with up to 50 cm long shoots. The leaves are short and oblong.

Brahmi is astringent, bitter, sweet, cooling and is considered to be good for digestion and generally strengthening. It is used to treat many diseases. Pharmacologically, Brahmi can have a soothing, muscle-relaxing, anti-inflammatory, antirheumatic, analgesic, anti-tumour and antioxidant effect.

Clinical studies show that the Brahmi adaptogen increases intelligence and reduces anxiety. It is an excellent nerve tonic from the perspective of evidence-based medicine and has a soothing effect. [5]

Brahmi also demonstrates a bronchodilatory, antiperspirant and analgesic effect. The analgesic effect is based on the Bacosin contained in Brahmi. [6]

---

[5] http://www.ncbi.nlm.nih.gov/pubmed/12957224
[6] http://www.ncbi.nlm.nih.gov/pmc/articles/PMC3506936/

Brahmi application and effect

Brahmi is taken in the form of freshly pressed juice (10 - 20ml), dried powder (3 - 5g) or root powder (500mg - 2g). In Ayurveda, it can also a be taken in a herbal drink made of ghee, honey or raw sugar and other herbs and fruits or a herbal wine. The effects of Brahmi in enhancing mental performance can be enhanced by taking inositol or a vitamin B complex at the same time.

As a lot of rosacea sufferers in the forums gave positive reports about Brahmi and Gotu kola, I found out more about them and decided to try the herbs themselves. [7]

The plants were delivered after a few days, of course looking a little sad after being transported, and I put them in pots in the garden, watering them generously each day. They also developed splendidly, and twice daily I picked about 5 leaves from 1-2 Brahmi twigs, and 1 Gotu Kola leaf daily, chewed them thoroughly and ate them. The slightly bitter taste can be well tolerated.

---

[7] You can order both herbs online at Rühlemann Pflanzenversand.

After the daily intake, I started to notice a slight improvement in my skin.

Turmeric (Curcuma longa)

Curcumin is found in the root of the plant turmeric. It is a component of curry spices, is used for colouring food and has long been appreciated and used in traditional medicine because of its antioxidant and anti-inflammatory effect. Curcumin inhibits the formation of metastases in advanced chest and prostate cancer, improves the pain symptoms and mobility in arthrosis, has a positive effects on diabetic complications and lowers the blood fat values (see Wikipedia, Curcuma). Curcuma is found in the curry spice and is available in capsules and as a tea.

Ginger (Zingiber officinale)

Ginger contains active phytonutrients, such as gingerol and shogaol, which have a strong anti-inflammatory effect.

Prepare a tea of fresh ginger. Simply peel a piece of ginger root and place a few slices in a cup, pour some boiling water into the cup and leave it for five minutes. rosacea forum participants report that this can lead to a weakening of the triggers for a rosacea attack. Once again, just try it out.

Liquorice root extract (Glycyrrhiza inflata)

Liquorice root extracts are traditionally used for the topical treatment of rosacea. In mild cases of rosacea, significant improvements can be seen over a period of several weeks with continuous use. Although liquorice can have many side effects, it has a soothing effect on rosacea and other skin diseases.

The flavonoid "Licochalcon A", obtained from the liquorice root, has been shown to inhibit the release of inflammatory substances and has an antibacterial and antiparasitic effect, with the pleasant consequence that redness of the skin also decreases. [8]

Essential oils are taking on the fight against rosacea: As the skin of rosacea sufferers is no longer flexible due to a chronic enlargement of the blood vessels and is therefore often dry because it cannot hold any moisture, the skin needs care using an oil which has a healing effect. For this purpose, pure almond, evening primrose or wild rose oil from organic cultivation can be tried, which should not be perfumed.

Rose hip oil is traditionally used for many skin problems. It can reduce the redness of the skin, and supports the development of healthy skin cells.

Geranium oil supports the lymphatic vessels and veins, and strengthens the skin's ability to fight infections, and it is reassuring at the same time.

---

[8] https://www.researchgate.net/publication/7225673_Anti-inflammato-ry_efficacy_of_Licochalcone_A_Correlation_of_clinical_potency_and_i n_vitro_effects

Tea tree oil (Malaleuca alternfolia)

Tea tree oil is a good antiseptic and an anti-inflammatory. It acts against microorganisms such as skin mites, and its antimicrobial properties protect the skin from rosacea by eliminating demodex parasites. Carefully administer some tea tree oil to the inflamed spots or pustules on your face using a cotton wool swab, not too close to the eyes. Apply it twice daily and observe the development. If too much is applied, an allergic contact dermatitis can develop, i.e. use moderately ...

Less common oils are oregano and borage oil:

Oregano oil (Origanum vulgare)

Essential oregano oil is a powerful natural antibiotic, which supposedly inhibits the formation of inflammatory messenger substances and can even kill hair follicle mites. In a recent study, it was found that Oregano is significantly better than all of the 18 currently used antibiotics for the treatment of MRSA staphylococci infections. [9]

---

[9] http://blogs.naturalnews.com/oregano-oil-powerful-plant-derived-antibiotic-antiseptic/

Borage oil (Borago officinalis)

Borage oil is extracted from the seeds of the Borage plant, which is also known as the star flower. The oil is mainly known for its skin-soothing and anti-inflammatory properties. It contains essential fatty acids, including gamma-linolenic acid, which is essential for the maintenance of the structure and flexibility of the cell membranes. The essential fatty acids in Borage oil help to regenerate the skin by promoting the growth of healthy skin cells. Simply apply a few drops of the oil on your clean and moisturised face and leave it to act.

The wax-like **Jojoba oil** moisturises the skin and forms a barrier against environmental influences and supports the reduction of swelling in the skin.

This list of herbal remedies is to serve as a stimulus. Although they are not officially recognised, they may be helpful, because when you are looking for effective remedies for rosacea, you have to do it on your own.

Other customary treatment methods

As skin affected by rosacea can react very sensitively to external chemicals and physical stimuli, as well as to some foods and drinks, it is necessary to know your own trigger factors and avoid them.

Each sufferer's skin responds to different trigger factors. In the course of time you will learn for yourself which products and situations you should avoid.

There are three different types of stimuli:

Chemical stimuli: Skin care products containing alcohol, soap or camphor, peels

Physical stimuli: Friction, solar radiation, saunas

Triggering food/drink: Spicy food, hot drinks, alcohol

Doctors prescribe creams and gels such as Metronidazole, Skinoren with azelaic acid and Soolantra with the insecticide Ivermectin for the first two stages of rosacea. The anti-inflammatory components should cause the rosacea to fade. If the creams do not work, antibiotics are prescribed at a low dosage, which can, however, promote bacterial antibiotic resistance and should therefore be reserved for severe forms of rosacea.

Isotretinoin is also used in severe and therapy-resistant pathologies. It has been marketed by Roche since 1982 under the name of Accutane and also works against hair follicle mites, but can lead to significant side effects such as irritation of the skin, mucous membrane and conjunctiva, headaches as well as liver function disorders, and it can possibly trigger depression.

Since 2014, the brimonidine gel Mirvaso by Galderma has been authorised for use in the EU as a symptomatic therapy for the treatment of redness in rosacea teleangiectatica. This contains a long-known alpha-2 receptor agonist, which has been used up to now in droplets, to reduce intraocular pressure in open-angle glaucoma. The stimulation of alpha-2 receptors leads to vasoconstriction and thus to poor circulation in the skin and a reduction of the redness in the face. However, the gel only fights the symptoms - not the cause of the disease, and does not have any effect on rosacea papulopustulosa.

The Ivermectin-containing ointment Soolantra by Galderma has been approved for the treatment of rosacea in Germany since 2015. It is used in adult patients for the topical treatment of inflammatory lesions of the (papulopustulous) rosacea. According to PD Dr. Jürgen Schauber, Department of Dermatology and Allergology, Ludwig-Maximilians University of Munich, Soolantra creme showed improved efficacy compared to the reference substance Metronidazole in clinical trials. demodex mites, which live in the hair roots and sebaceous glands in nearly all adults, are believed to release bacteria into the skin, especially when they die, which causes skin inflammation. Ivermectin is anti-inflammatory and antiparasitic.

Corticosteroids should not be used against rosacea as they increase the symptoms.

Antibiotics

Tetracyclines can be very effective when taken over several weeks. The effective mechanism of tetracycline is not yet fully clear. It has an anti-inflammatory effect, which is not linked to the antibacterial effect. However, relapses can occur within a few weeks after the treatment has ended.

As rosacea, if it affects the eye, can lead to permanent eye damage such as corneal opacity, regular eye examinations should be performed if the eyes are affected, and tetracyclines are the selected medicine until the symptoms disappear.

Laser

Many people with rosacea regularly receive laser treatment to the reddened areas of the face. This treatment removes the red veins permanently. The dilated blood vessels are closed and faded. Laser therapy for rosacea is not yet paid for by the statutory health insurance providers, but by most private insurance providers (between approx. €50 to approx. €300 per session depending on the treatment area, therapy centre and time expenditure).

The initial stage of rosacea, which is characterised by redness and vessel enlargement (couperosis, telangiectasia), is best addressed using light and laser therapies. The green light of the 532nm-KTP neodymium YAG laser, which can target superficial vessel dilatations (typical red cheeks), is apparently very effective. At this stage, IPL systems (these are not LASERs) and the **pulsed dye laser** can be used successfully. [10]

A rhyniophyte (nodal nasal disease) can be treated either by operative ablation using a scalpel or a focused CO_2 laser.

Ichthyol

Ichthyol (chemical: ammonium bituminosulfonate) is a sulphur-containing shale oil and smells like tar. In contrast to tar products, however, it is not suspected of being carcinogenic or mutagenic. Its antibacterial effect can reduce the papules, inflammation and pustules. At the same time, Ichthyol also acts against fungi. In the event of prolonged treatment, however, there may also be a reduction in the effect. (Source: R. Engst: Dark shale oils are the basis

---

[10] http://www.hautsache.de/Rosazea/Lasertherapie/Teil-I-Grundlagen-der-Lasertherapie.php

for an effective dermatosis, in the hospital newspaper of the Davos Alexander Hospital 3/1999, p. 15 f.)

The German company Ichthyol produces Ichthraletten tablets, which you can order online without a prescription. I have taken them myself. 2-2-2 for the first 2 weeks, then 1-1-1. It is best to buy 2 packs of 60 tablets. You need to have a lot of patience and take them regularly for a long time, until an inflammation-minimizing effect is shown.

Lidocaine

A new approach is the use of lidocaine, which is usually used for local anaesthesia. Recent laboratory studies have shown that lidocaine can be a promising agent for if staphylococci is part of the rosacea disorder, as it can inhibit the inflammation caused by its toxins.

Endolysin staphefekt

The creams and gels of the brand Gladskin with the bacteriophage-derived endolysin staphefekt are directed against staphylococci and specifically destroy the cell envelopes of Staphylococcus aureus, causing the bacteria to burst. For example, endolysins are used against gram-positive bacteria on mucous membranes.

Nutrition tips

Which foods support healthy skin?

Vitamin C helps to produce collagen, which ensures elastic skin. Good sources are citrus fruits, watermelons, grapes, tomatoes and green salads and vegetables, as well as avocados. Vitamin A supports skin repair and is found mainly in orange, red and yellow fruits and vegetables such as mangoes, and green vegetables.

Another nutrient for healthy skin is the anti-inflammatory omega-3 fatty acid, which can be found, for example, in linseed, chia and hemp seeds, walnuts and fatty fish such as wild salmon. Spices such as coriander, cardamom, saffron and fennel are also regarded as soothing.

Ayurveda experts recommend salmon, goat's cheese, mild vegetables and turmeric. Whether grain crops such as oats, germinated wheat bread, barley, granola, amaranth, white rice and tapioca are helpful, still needs to be tested. [11]

---

[11] http://www.byrdie.co.uk/rosacea-diet

An anti-inflammatory diet can reduce the symptoms of rosacea. Avoid inflammation-promoting foods such as industrially processed foods, sugars, refined oils and wheat, and instead incorporate natural coconut oil, vegetables, and avocado into your diet.

A ketogenic diet is anti-inflammatory

A ketogenic diet can be helpful for all patients suffering from diseases related to inflammatory processes in the body. A diet rich in sugars or carbohydrates negatively influences these inflammatory processes. Reducing or, even better, giving up sugar and carbohydrates (bread, rice, noodles, potatoes) can reduce inflammation, and this was the case for me.

Meanwhile, cancer patients also rely on the effect of the fat-rich diet, which regulates the blood glucose level. A permanently low blood glucose level results in less insulin (growth hormone) being released and prevents tumours from growing rapidly.

The main part of the energy supply in this diet are high-quality oils and fats. About 70% of the calories, up to 200 g fat, should be consumed daily. The most suitable fats are butter, virgin coconut oil and olive oil.

Try my recipe for a delicious coffee similar to the well-known "bullet-proof coffee": put a big cup of hot coconut oil and one tablespoon of coffee with a heaped teaspoon of butter or 2 tablespoons liquid cream into a blender and mix. It tastes like a creamy latte macchiato.

Two teaspoons of high quality coconut oil daily have a germicidal and antifungal effect. If you are not used to coconut oil, you can start with just a teaspoon, so that the body can accustom itself to the unfamiliar fatty food. If you take too much, 'Montezuma's revenge' might catch you, because coconut oil can lead to diarrhoea when taken in unusual amounts.

Probiotics

Some international studies show a link between the use of probiotics and an improvement in rosacea and acne symptoms. Probiotics are microorganisms - essentially lactic acid and bifidobacteria - which enter the intestine with food, settle there and thus achieve positive health effects.1) In a Korean study, 56 patients were able to improve their skin by drinking fermented Lactobacillus. In an Italian study, half of the patients received probiotic food supplements in combination with the standard treatment. The other half of the patients received no probiotic supplement. Improvements in the symptoms of acne and rosacea only occurred in the probiotic comparison group.

Although there are other studies that confirm the positive aspects of probiotics, it is anticipated that in the near future innovative probiotic products can be expected for the treatment of rosacea.[12][13]

Probiotics ensure a healthy intestinal flora, counteract inflammation and thus support the healing of rosacea

---

[12]https://www.aad.org/media/news-releases/could-probiotics-be-the-next-big-thing-in-acne-and-rosacea-treatments

[13] http://wirtschaft.saarland.de/SID-C51B4B99-C51F98FA/6031.htm
Thanks to Ulli Buttgereit for the link!

symptoms. Try natural yoghurt, sauerkraut and other fermented foods, or even lactic acid cultures in capsules.[14]

Externally applied probiotics, for example, in the form of a face mask of yogurt and turmeric and honey, a serum or a lotion, can also restore the balance of the bacteria on the skin surface and thus contribute to treatment.

Water fasting

It is becoming increasingly apparent that intermittent fasting for a fixed time is healthy in addition to regular sleeping hours at night. Breakfast in English-speaking regions is called "breakfast" because the night fast is broken in the morning with the breakfast. You can simply extend the night fast by a few hours, drink a few glasses of water in the morning and have breakfast later, or eliminate breakfast completely. The old beliefs, which require a rich breakfast for a successful day, have long been left behind. It is even healthy to fast for a whole day, or even two days,

---

[14] http://blog.yeswellness.com/probiotics-food-is-the-secret-to-treat-skin-conditions

from time to time. Today, many people follow the 2+5 method: 2 days fasting per week. This does not harm anybody, on the contrary: the body is treated with a break from constant food and, as long as you do not eat too much during the remaining days to compensate for the "lost" days, you will even lose weight. Even our ancestors did not always have enough to eat and were not served by a refrigerator which was always well-filled. Our bodies are thus prepared for periods of scarcity and can compensate for them due to available fat reserves.

Anti-redness tea

Drink medicinal teas, such as peppermint, chamomile and green tea, and try some tea compresses: simply allow several bags to stand for 10 minutes in a pot of boiling water and allow the liquid to cool in the refrigerator. Pour the tea onto a washcloth and squeeze it onto the face for up to one minute. Repeat this one to two times a day. The polyphenols in the green tea have skin-rejuvenating properties, and chamomile and peppermint teas benefit every kind of facial redness.

Sea fish oil capsules

Our diet often contains too much saturated fat, while fish contain polyunsaturated omega-3 fatty acids, which are very healthy for the body. A large part of the diet of the Greenlanders consists of sea fish. The omega-3 fatty acid docosahexaenoic acid (DHA) and eicosapentaenoic acid (EPA) cannot be formed by the body itself if the corresponding precursors are not present. But not everyone can eat fish, or wants to eat fish, at least twice a week. This is why it is a good to supply the body with sufficient and regular amounts of these important polyunsaturated omega-3 fatty acids in capsule form, in addition to food.

Omega-6 fatty acids can be helpful, but only when they are taken in equilibrium with Omega-3. Excessive omega-6 intake leads to rosacea. Some excellent natural combined omega-6 and omega-3 sources are all kinds of nuts and seeds, such as brazil nuts, walnuts, pistachios, sesame seeds and linseed. Peanut butter and tahini also ensures a balanced supply.

Lemon juice

A basic diet is also considered helpful for rosacea. A daily glass of water with a squeezed lemon can be beneficial. Three times daily, one to two tablespoons of natural apple cider vinegar in a glass of water have a similar effect, protecting against hyperacidity and positively supporting the balance of the intestinal flora, so that even yeast fungi such as Candida cannot reproduce so easily. Candida albicans can generally be found in the majority of healthy people, mainly superficially on the skin or mucous membrane. If the immune system is weakened, however, it can lead to candidiasis, infection of the skin, the mucous membranes or the internal organs with a Candida yeast fungus.

Nicotinamide (vitamin B3),

is mainly found in meat, fish and offal. A good vegetable source of vitamin B3 supplier is pure ground coffee. The vitamin supports many metabolic processes in the body, for example the production of fatty acids. Vitamin B3 belongs to the group of water soluble B vitamins, and it protects against non-melanoma-induced skin tumours caused by UV radiation. This is indicated by the results of a clinical study presented in 2015 by Australian scientists at the American Society of Clinical Oncology Congress in Chicago. Current literature shows that the B vitamin supports the brain, the health of the pancreas and the joints.

To reduce skin inflammation, take 500 mg twice daily. Caution: Do not confuse with niacin! Niacin produces redness and inflammation, and nicotinamide acts as a preventive measure. Anything which increases blood circulation should be avoided.

Soothing agents

There are some agents which you can try. Because we are dealing with mites, you can try **using** lice shampoo against the itching: wash your face with lice shampoo. Leave on your face for 10 minutes, then rinse off.

Honey

The ancient Egyptians used honey for therapeutic baths, and Cleopatra seduced men by using extensive beauty treatments with honey and fragrant essences.

A beauty editor with rosacea wanted to try the effects herself, so she bought a jar of organic honey. She spread a thin layer of honey on her face in the evening, left the mask to work for thirty minutes, then rinsed it off. She immediately noticed a pleasing difference in the softness of her cheeks. Within a week, the honey facial mask helped her skin to regain its pH balance, the redness faded away, and the small bumps disappeared.[15]

---

[15] https://www.yahoo.com/beauty/can-honey-cure-rosacea-one-beauty-editor-says-yes-129597962188.html

Cucumber as a cooling remedy

Cucumber is a component of many creams and lotions thanks to its astringent, cooling and moisturising properties. Cucumber pulp mainly consists of water, but also contains the vitamins A, C, E and caffeic acid, which together help to soothe the skin and reduce swelling. Therefore, the old cosmetic trick of laying cucumber slices on the eyelids helps to relieve swelling. The peel contains beneficial minerals such as magnesium, potassium and silicic acid. Silica is an important component of healthy connective tissue, which makes the skin look clear and radiant. rosacea sufferers can try using cucumber masks: puree the cucumber and mix it with yoghurt, then apply to the skin. Or simply use cucumber slices.[16]

Healing earth masks are also effective, as they have an antibacterial and anti-inflammatory effect.

If, as in 30-50% of rosacea cases, the edges of the eyelids are also affected, the eyelashes can be carefully

---

[16] http://itapuranga.com.br/why-cucumber-is-a-cool-rosacea-remedy/

wiped in the evening with **tea tree oil** on a cotton wool swab.

You should **change your pillow daily**, or turn your pillow over after one night and change after the second night.

Encasing quilt covers **for the bedding are highly recommended.** They are so tightly woven that they are mite-dense, meaning that mites and their residues are kept away from the skin. It is best to wash it in the washing machine before use so that the cover does not crackle.

Here are links to the encasings that I use:

TAURO 24185 Top cover encasing mite dust-tight, compact fibre structure made of microfilaments, free of harmful substances, 135 x 200 cm [17]

TAURO 24147 Pillow cover encasing mite dust-tight, compact fibre structure made of microfilaments, free of harmful substances, 80 x 80 cm. [18]

---

[17] http://www.amazon.de/dp/B006MCTZ56
[18] http://www.amazon.de/dp/B006MCTZA6

Take the test!

You can very easily test yourself to see whether your skin is colonized by hair follicle mites.

For this you need a microscope with a magnification of at least 40x, and glass slides (available online), as well as some vegetable oil. It can be a very simple microscope, but there should be a light supply under the slide. In addition, you will need a tool to scrape the sebum from the skin. The metal handle of a teaspoon can be used as a hand scraper, for example, or another flat metal implement with a tip. It should be possible to press the tool on the skin and wipe it without cutting it into the skin.

Take a glass slide and drip a droplet of oil into the middle of it. Then, press the top and sides of a nostril so tightly that sebum swells out. Collect this sebum using the tool, and place it in the oil on the slide. Mix the sebum with the oil and observe the mixture under the microscope. You will see many dead skin cells and other things that you have scraped off the skin. If mites are present, you will be able to see them immediately.

Have patience as soon as you have tried it, you will realize how easy it is. If no mites can be seen in the nasal sebum, press the skin between the eyebrows and between the lower lip and the chin, mix the resulting sebum with a new droplet of oil and examine under the microscope.

For comparison, here you will find two microscope photos of demodex hair follicle mites. On the first photo, you can see a single mite in 400x magnification:

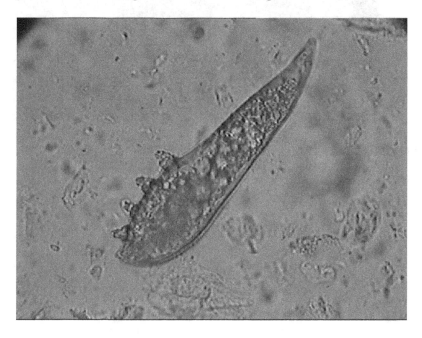

Image source: Dominik Golenhofen, Alternative Practitioner

The second photo shows the outline of two nymphs and an egg:

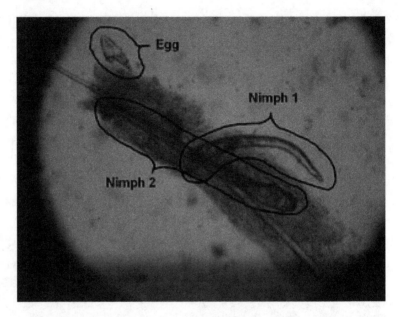

Image source: Dominik Golenhofen, Alternative Practitioner

An effective weapon

The most important aid in the fight against rosacea is a facial cream that kills demodex mites. After researching online for a long time, and searching the records in international forums, I ended up on a Chinese website (www.demodexsolutions.com), where a Chinese professor had been researching the subject of rosacea for 40 years and developed a cream which has been clinically tested and patented, and has proven to be effective in killing demodex mites and bacteria. According to him, after applying the cream, the skin recovers from symptoms associated with rosacea and acne, such as inflammation, and becomes smooth, soft and healthy again. After my already doubtful journey so far, I thought, what harm could it cause, and ordered the ZZ cream (Zhongzhou Zinc oxide and sublimed sulphur ointment), which was not cheap.

The cream arrived a few days after I had made the order. The silver pot looked trustworthy, with a hygienic protective cover over the cream. When I opened it, a menthol-like smell reached up to my nose. First, I washed my face and hands with warm water and a neutral soap. Then, with a finger, I placed a few dots of the white and relatively dry concentrated cream on my facial skin, rubbing it in gently, while avoiding my eyes and mouth. I repeated this process in the morning and in the evening. After the application, my skin condition improved after just one day. At first, it is possible that the skin will "peel off". This is a symptom of healing, because healthy skin then appears from underneath.

You should be patient with the treatment, because even though the symptoms may disappear quickly, treatment with the cream should continue **consistently for 4 months**, because the long mites, (demodex folliculorum[19]), can all be removed after 3 months, but the short ones (demodex brevis[20]) are not as easy to reach. It takes 4 months until they are all actually dead. If the treatment stops sooner, some mites may still live, multiply and spread again. A 20g jar is sufficient for several weeks.

After the first week of treatment, my skin became very dry, so I applied a little Toleriane cream from Roche

---

[19] https://en.wikipedia.org/wiki/Demodex_folliculorum
[20] https://de.wikipedia.org/wiki/Demodex_brevis

Posay over the very dry spots (nasolabial folds). So that the layer of the ZZ cream is thin, you can moisten the facial skin a bit and apply the cream in a thinner layer.

After successful completion of the treatment, it is advisable to apply the cream at least once a week in the evening to keep the mites in check. If, after some time, you feel that your skin condition deteriorates, apply it occasionally until you notice an improvement, for example, only in the evening. You will have to discover the most appropriate method for your own skin. In any case, it is great that those affected by rosacea finally have a strong ally with this cream, which can successfully take up the fight against their suffering.[21]

Composition of the ZZ cream: The Zhongzhou Zinc oxide and sublimed sulphur ointment is a mixture of Western and Chinese medicine and is protected by a secret Chinese state patent. It has no side effects, and it does not contain any harmful substances such as pesticides, lead, gasoline, mercury, hormones, steroids, cortisone and so on.

---

[21] Here are some references from people who have used the cream to look at and read:
http://www.demodexsolutions.com/phpbb3/viewforum.php?f=9

No toxic and/or harmful effects are observed during a longer application period.

Ingredients of ZZ Cream:

The ointment formula is protected by a Chinese patent, and here is a list of some ingredients:

- Zinc oxide
- Sublimed sulphur
- Menthol
- Salicylic acid
- Chinese medicinal herbs
- The ointment base, which is based on a complex formula.

As unfortunately I did not take any before-after pictures of myself, I asked the German distributers of ZZ cream (in Germany called DemoDerm cream) if they could provide me with pictures to show the effects of the cream. They kindly sent me the three following clear before-after examples:

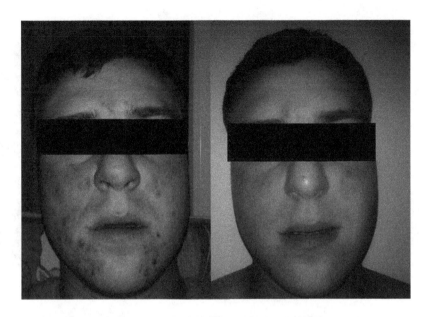

Source of pictures from pages 55 and 56: Dominik Golenhofen, Alternative Practitioner, www.demodex.de

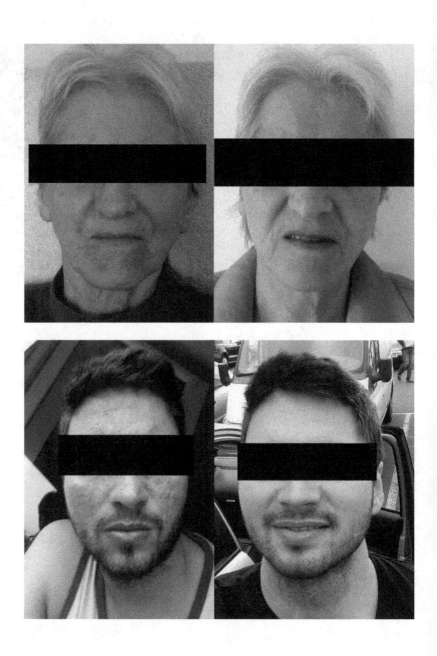

Skin care

Facial skin affected by rosacea is very irritable and sensitive, so it should be treated only with very mild products. As the skin barrier is already damaged, the cleansing agents should not contain foamy surfactants or detergents, and facial lotions must be perfume-free and not too greasy, in order to prevent the pores from becoming clogged. It is advisable to always pay attention to UV protection in the daily cream. Do not forget to use sun cream with a higher sunlight protection factor, as well as allergy protection, when outside in the sun! As 90 percent of ultraviolet rays penetrate through the cloud cover, we are unknowingly exposed to harmful UV rays without protection. Only dab your face lightly after washing, and do not rub off. Of course, peelings as well as microdermabrasion should be avoided, as they are poison for the already inflamed skin. Products with retina and glycolic acid are also a no-go. Light make-up can be used to conceal the inflammation until the skin has healed.

After the painstaking trial of many expensive face creams from the pharmacies, which either led to irritation or even more redness, I found the "LA MER" series from ESTÉE LAUDER.

I had previously heard of the luxury miracle cream "LA MER", but because of the high price, I had always hesitated to buy it. After a sample came into my hands by chance, I was instantly impressed by its soothing effect and the fine fragrance. My skin really seemed to have been waiting for this cream. My face sucked in the cream like a sponge, and became clearer and finer-pored. First, I tried the original "CRÈME DE LA MER", which resembles Nivea cream a little in its consistency. It was a bit too rich and heavy. "THE MOISTURIZING SOFT CREME", which I like to use in the evening, is a little smoother and easier to apply. During the day, "THE MOISTURIZING LOTION" is sufficient, and in summer, "THE OIL ABSORBING LOTION". Applying a few drops of "The Miracle Oil" before the lotion offers an even more luxurious treatment, and the skin feels reborn. Generally, rosacea sufferers should take care when applying the cream, not to 'paste' it too thickly over the skin so that it cannot breathe, otherwise the skin will react badly.

It is important, as already mentioned above, to use good sun protection, especially on the face, with at least light protection factor 15, though a higher factor is better. For facial protection, I like to use the matt Sunfluid lotion for sensitive skin by Eucerin with sun protection factor 50. Although it is not cheap (about 15 euros), the face is well protected and does not become shiny. For the body, I use Ladival sun protection gel for allergic skin with light protection factor 50, without perfume, fats or colourings. It is not a gel, but a pleasant milk lotion.

It is self-explanatory that sensitive skin should not be additionally irritated by peelings, coarse cloths or sponges!

Use hand-warm water to clean the skin. Hot water dries the skin, while cold stimulates the blood circulation and can lead to a flare-up of rosacea.

Shaving tips for men with rosacea

Although rosacea is diagnosed up to three times more frequently in women, men with rosacea have to struggle with a particular challenge of their own, because shaving often leads to irritation and increases skin problems. Here are a few shaving tips for rosacea patients with sensitive skin.

• Consider the use of an electric shaver to avoid skin irritation caused by blunt razor blades.

• Give yourself enough time to shave. Shaving too hastily increases the chance of shaving, scratches and cuts.

• If you prefer shaving with a disposable blade, remember to replace the blades after using five or six times.

• Clean and moisten the skin before shaving. Use mild shaving creams or lotions which do not burn your skin. If you prefer not to moisturise your skin, gently clean your face with warm water. Foam the skin with shaving cream or gel and allow it to penetrate the skin for one or two minutes before shaving. Keep the skin moist and warm during shaving, and remember to always shave in the hair growth direction. Be very gentle and take a lot of time for the problem areas.

• Wash your face immediately after shaving with lukewarm water to prevent possible inflammation. Apply a shaving balm or moisturiser to soothe the skin.[22][23]

Perform the mineral oil check!

Paraffin/silicones are petroleum products, which are used as a fat and cream base in many cosmetic products. They should be avoided by sufferers of rosacea, as they close the pores in the same manner as a plastic bag, and thus prevent the skin from being able to breathe.

University studies have shown that the water-insoluble paraffin's attack the protective acid layer of the skin, therefore depriving it of its natural protection. After this substance has been applied, very scaly skin usually results.

So make sure you perform a mineral oil check by looking

---

[22] https://www.rosacea.org/weblog/shaving-tips-men-rosacea
[23] http://www.menshealth.de/artikel/tipps-fuer-eine-perfekte-rasur.236.html

through the list of ingredients, or use natural cosmetics, which do not contain paraffin.

Always check the ingredients of your skin care products f you suffer from rosacea, especially to make sure they don't contain glycolic acid or retinoid. Even a strong brand such as Clinique contains cortisone, which makes the skin thinner when used for a long time, and Eucerin contains octinoxate, a light protection factor which makes the skin age faster. Dermatological products contain silicone which, like petroleum, form a plastic-like barrier and degrade the condition of the skin. [24]

Make-up:

Colour correction scheme for daily make-up:

- Green neutralises redness
- Yellow easily corrects redness and works against purple/blue skin tones
- Purple mildens dull yellow undertones in light skin

[24]   https://www.linkedin.com/pulse/review-top-3-rosacea-lotions-ingredients-hampton-skin-care

- Pink brightens dull light skin
- Orange diminishes dark circles and brown spots
- Blue neutralises pallor and excessive pigmentation of lighter skin

As an accompanying therapy, special massages, as well as methods for stress management, can be suitable if the skin is not too inflamed. You should simply try things out and find out what works best for you.

A final word

I am happy that I have been able share my knowledge with you, and now I am keeping my fingers crossed for a successful extermination of the demodex beasts, so you can keep your rosacea in check!

You are welcome to post your progress and new insights to my Facebook page[25] and share more tips with all readers.

With kind regards,

To a permanently youthful healthy and beautiful skin!

Yours,

Sylvia Lermann

---

[25] https://www.facebook.com/Rosazea.im.Griff/

CPSIA information can be obtained
at www.ICGtesting.com
Printed in the USA
BVHW091050040521
606339BV00006BB/1191